Voyager
Passport C

4

Fluency

ISBN 978-1-4168-0366-9

Printed in the United States of America   07 08 09 10 11 12 13   CMM   9 8 7 6 5 4 3 2 1

Table of Contents

Fluency Practice

 Read the story to each other.

 Read the story on your own.

 Read the story to your partner again. Try to read the story even better.

 Questions? Ask your partner two questions about the story. Tell each other about the story you just read.

Timed Reading

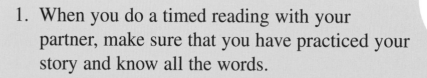

1. When you do a timed reading with your partner, make sure that you have practiced your story and know all the words.

2. When you are ready, tell your partner to start the timer.

3. Read carefully, and your partner will stop you at 1 minute. When you stop, mark your place.

4. Count the total number of words you read.

5. In the back of your Student Book, write the number of words you read and color in the squares on your Fluency Chart.

6. Now switch with your partner.

Twirling

The girl was the first in line at the shop. She had saved for months and had her cash in her purse. She wanted a baton so she could learn to twirl and lead the band. She asked the clerk for the baton.

He turned and said, "We are out." The girl was on the verge of tears.

Then a man came in with a box. "I have a return," he said.

The clerk opened the box, and there was a baton. The girl got the baton and learned to twirl and whirl it. Now she leads the band!⑨⑨

Baseball

Baseball is a fun game to play. It has many rules to learn. Here are a few facts about it.

- It is played with a bat and ball by two teams of nine players on a field.
- Each team takes turns in the field and at bat.
- The team batting tries to hit the ball so that they can run all the bases and score.
- The team with the most runs at the end of the game wins.

Would you like to know more? There are many good books about baseball in the library. Go have a look! ⑱

Ice-Skating

Sam watched Trish glide over the ice. She jumped and twirled without slipping. Sam wished he could skate. Trish skated up and sat for a quick rest. "Come skate Sam," she said.

"I do not know how," he told her.

Trish said she would teach Sam. He pulled on skates and laced them up. The two stepped out on the ice. Sam took a step and fell. But he got up. He hung onto Trish and took more steps. She helped him, and he crossed the ice. He went faster. He was skating!

Now Sam and Trish skate each day.⑩⓪

Joan and Nan

Joan lived on a farm with her pet goat Nan. Each day she fed Nan toast and oats and brushed her coat. Then they would walk up the road.

One day they went out to roam and walked all the way to the tall bridge by the ridge. They started across when Nan came to a halt. "Come on," said Joan, but the goat would not budge because she was scared. They had to get home!

Then Joan felt something in her coat. She had a bit of fudge. With one whiff, the goat turned and walked home with Joan!⑩⑩

Farms

There are many different kinds of farms. Some are small, and some are large.

Some grow crops such as hay, grain, soy beans, oats, greens, or corn. Crops are planted in the soil and grow. They are used for food.

Some farms raise animals. In the barn or yard, you may find goats, sheep, pigs, chicks, or cows. Animal farms may get paid for eggs, milk, or cheese or even goat or sheep hair to make wool.

Other farms grow the fruit that we eat such as plums, grapes, or pears. What kind of farm would you like to see?⑩⑩

Phil and the Farm

Phil spent each June with Gramps on the farm. He helped round up the animals with the old hound dog and worked on the grounds. But what he liked best was fishing with Gramps. For years he went to the brook to try to catch the big trout, but it always found a way off the hook. Still, it was fun, so off they went.

He sat on the ground and tossed out his line. As he was looking up at the clouds, he felt a tug. He had hooked the big trout! Gramps was so proud he took a photo. ⑩⑪

Talking to Animals

Meow! Woof! Chirp! You think your pet is trying to tell you something. What is it? People are solving the problem of how to talk with animals.

Dr. Irene Pepperberg works with Alex. He is an African Grey Parrot. Alex cannot say words.㊸ But Dr. Pepperberg says Alex knows what people say. Alex knows colors and shapes. He can even count to six.

Koko is a gorilla. Her teachers ask her questions. Koko answers with her hands. She uses sign language. Koko even makes up words when she does not know the right ones. Can you guess what Koko called an eye hat? That was her name for a mask.

Thanks, Champ

36"36

"Come on, Champ. It's time to go." Champ stood still while I put the Guide Dog vest on his back. Tears stung my eyes. "Does Champ have to go?" I asked Mom.㉜

"Rosa, this is the day we've been working for," Mom replied. "I know it's hard to say good-bye. But we have solved a problem for someone who cannot see. We have helped train Champ. He will be a great guide for a blind person."⑦⑦

A few weeks later, a letter came in the mail. It was from a man named Mark. A friend wrote the letter for him because Mark couldn't see. The letter told how Champ had changed Mark's life. With Champ's  help, Mark was able to do more things. I felt proud to have been a part of something so important.⑬⑥

"Way to go, Champ!" I said to myself.

The Ocean Test

Sam ice-skated on the frozen pond by her house. "It would be fun to skate on the huge, frozen ocean," she thought. "I've never seen ice at the beach. I wonder why."

Sam's dad helped her do a test. Sam filled two cups with water. She put salt in one and named it "ocean water." She filled the other cup with water from the pond.⑯ Sam put the cups in the freezer. Each hour Sam checked the cups. One cup of water froze quickly. Can you guess which one?

"Now you see, Sam," said Dad. "The salt in the ocean makes it harder for the water to freeze. It has to get very, very cold for ocean water to freeze."

"Aha!" said Sam. "That's why I don't see ice at the beach."

A Friend of the Animals

What would happen if you took worms to bed? What would your mother do? Jane Goodall took worms to bed. She was only a year old. Her mother did not yell. She knew Jane loved animals. She knew Jane wanted to learn about how worms move without legs.

Jane always knew that she wanted to learn about animals. She wanted to go to Africa to learn about chimps. But how could she? It was the 1950s. She was a young woman. She did not have enough money. Jane's mother said, "If you really want something, you work hard. You never give up. You will find a way." ⑩⑦

Jane did find a way. She worked and paid for her trip to Africa. Jane learned a lot about chimps. She learned that they can make tools. Before Jane, people thought that only we could think and make tools. Jane watched chimps pull leaves off sticks. They used the sticks as tools to get bugs out of the ground. Jane still is learning about chimps. She teaches us about them too.

Horse Hooves that Help

Look, Dad! There's a horse in the mall! You might find yourself saying these words soon. Small horses are being trained to help people who cannot see. There are many reasons for using horses as guides.

Many people know about guide dogs. They have solved many problems faced by people who are blind. But some people who cannot see are unable to be around dogs. They sneeze and cough when dogs are near. Most people do not have this problem with horses.⑧²

Some people who are blind are scared of dogs. Guide dogs are large. Guide horses are much smaller. They are about 26 inches tall. That's about as tall as your desk. Many people who are scared of large dogs are not scared of the small guide horses.

Can you see behind you? Horses can! Their eyes are on the sides of their head. That means they can see almost all the way around without having to turn their head. They also can see well at night.

Guide horses are calm. They are able to learn quickly. They can be "eyes" for someone who cannot see. Do not be surprised if you see a small horse in a mall near you!

Help from Dolphins

Would you like to swim with a dolphin? Would you like to hold on to its fin and let it pull you through the water? How do you think its skin would feel? Many people are answering these questions and solving some problems at the same time.

For years, people have told of ways dolphins help them. People on boats have told of dolphins guiding them to land. People swimming in the sea have told of dolphins helping them get out of the water safely. Now dolphins are helping people solve different kinds of problems.

Dolphins are being used as medicine. People who are sick are swimming with dolphins. Some doctors think the dolphins help heal the people. Dolphins help people who have problems learning too.⑫⑥

They may have problems talking. These people swim with the dolphins. Then they are able to talk more or to learn better. Some doctors think this is because the people are happy to be with the dolphins. Their brains work harder. They learn better.

Some people are using dolphins to solve other problems. Dolphins do not use ears like we do. They send out sounds in waves. These sounds bounce off things in front of the dolphins. The sounds come back to the dolphins. This is how they "hear." Scientists are using this idea to help people who cannot hear.

Dolphins are playful and loving. They like people. They are helping us solve many different problems.

An Important Flight

No one had ever flown a plane across the Atlantic Ocean alone. In 1927, Charles Lindbergh thought he should try.

Charles packed four sandwiches and two bottles of water. He got 451 gallons of gas. On May 20, 1927, he took off from New York.

Charles flew all day. He flew all night. Sometimes he couldn't see. It was hard to stay awake. He flew in cold rain.

Charles thought he should turn around and fly back to New York. But he decided to keep going.⑧⑥

At last, Charles saw fishing boats. He knew he was close to land. He saw the lights of a city. It was Paris, France. He had been flying for more than 33 hours.

More than 100,000 people were waiting and looking for the plane. Charles landed the plane. He had made it! He opened the door of the plane and stepped out. People ran to Charles. They crowded around him. Police had to carry him through the cheering people.

Charles was a hero!

Earth's Star

Look up in the sky. Do you see the sun? Did you know the sun is a star? The sun doesn't look like the stars we see at night because it is closer to Earth than they are. Yet the sun is still very far away.

We use the sun to help us tell time. As Earth turns, the sun seems to be in different places in the sky.⑥⑨ In the morning, we see the sun in the eastern part of the sky. At noon, the sun is high over our heads. In the evening, we watch the sun set in the west. We know it is night when there is very little light, and we can't see the sun at all.

Word List

know	way
question	could
how	only
someone	work
beach	people
you	more